ORIGAMI **FLOWERS**

ORIGAMI FLOWERS

SOONBOKE SMITH

STERLING PUBLISHING CO., INC.
NEW YORK
A Sterling/Chapelle Book

Chapelle, Ltd.
Jo Packham • Sara Toliver • Cindy Stoeckl

Editor: Karmen Quinney

Book Design: Renato Stanisic

Photostylist: Suzy Skadburg

Photographer: Ryne Hazen for Hazen Photography

If you have questions or comments, please contact:
Chapelle, Ltd., Inc.,
P.O. Box 9252, Ogden, UT 84409
(801) 621-2777 • (801) 621-2788 Fax
e-mail: chapelle@chapelleltd.com
Web site: chapelleltd.com

Library of Congress Cataloging-in-Publication Data
Smith, Soonboke.
    Origami flowers/Soonboke Smith.
        p. cm.
    "A Sterling/Chapelle Book."
    Includes index.
    ISBN 1-4027-1483-1
    1. Origami. 2. Flowers in art. I. Title
    TT870.S572 2005
    736'. 982--dc22   2004024487

10 9 8 7 6 5 4 3 2

Published by Sterling Publishing Co., Inc.
387 Park Avenue South, New York, NY 10016
©2005 by Soonboke Smith
Distributed in Canada by Sterling Publishing,
⅟ Canadian Manda Group, 165 Dufferin Street,
Toronto, Ontario, Canada M6K 3H6
Distributed in the United Kingdom by GMC Distribution Services,
Castle Place, 166 High Street, Lewes, East Sussex, England BN7 1XU
Distributed in Australia by Capricorn Link (Australia) Pty. Ltd.,
P.O. Box 704, Windsor, NSW 2756, Australia
Printed in China
All Rights Reserved

Sterling ISBN-13: 978-1-4027-1483-2
        ISBN-10: 1-4027-1483-1

For information about custom editions, special sales, premium and
corporate purchases, please contact Sterling Special Sales
Department at 800-805-5489 or specialsales@sterlingpub.com.

CONTENTS

INTRODUCTION 8

GENERAL INSTRUCTIONS 10

BLOOMING PETALS 30

GIVING THANKS 32

POPPIES FOREVER 34

PURPLE STARS 36

PERFECT PEONIES 38

CRAZY COSMOS 42

STAR FLOWER 45

PINWHEEL DAISIES 47

SWEET CARNATIONS 50

FLOWER FIREWORKS 53

CUTE CLOVERS 56

BLOOMING FLOWERS 58

ELEGANT IRISES 60

LOVELY LILIES 63

BEAUTIFUL BLOSSOMS 64

CHARMING ANEMONIES 66

COLOR SPOTS 69

PRETTY PETALS 72

SPRING TULIPS 74

DELICATE BELLFLOWERS 77

Vivid Violets 80

Morning Glories 82

Periwinkle Patch 85

Periwinkle Adaptation 89

Starburst Dahlias 90

Orange Twinkles 93

Enchanting Posies 96

Blooming Starfish 99

Cyclamen Flowers 102

Cyclamen Buds 105

Petunia Kaleidoscope 106

Morning Glories II 109

Potted Pansies 111

Rose Bouquet 115

Sunshine Lilies 120

METRIC CONVERSION CHART 126

INDEX 127

INTRODUCTION

For centuries, there were no written directions for folding origami models. The directions were taught to each generation, then handed down to the next, then the next. The art of origami flowers has become part of the cultural heritage of the Korean people from their daily life to their special celebrations.

The art of paper folding began long before paper was invented. Asian and Polynesian peoples are known to have created ceremonial and utilitarian handicrafts by folding and weaving ti leaves, palm fronds, and pounded mulberry bark.

It is only in the last 200 years, as people from Asia emigrated to the west, that the ancient art of paper folding, as well as other traditional Asian arts and crafts, made its appearance in Europe and America.

The art of folding paper has become more diverse in its artistic complexity as world cultures have begun to mingle in the last century. In the West, the art of folding paper is more commonly known as "origami," the Japanese word for folding paper. The word origami lends itself to the almost magical metamorphosis that paper undergoes as it is folded into fanciful shapes. Origami literally translates into paper (ori) and magical spirit (gami or kami). The magical quality of folding paper into enchanting objects makes origami a powerful educational and therapeutic tool. Schoolteachers use origami as a fun way to teach subjects like geometry, science, and oriental culture. Physical therapists use origami to help clients develop hand strength and fine hand motor skills. Counseling therapists use origami to teach clients relaxation techniques and also to break the ice with those who are reluctant to interact.

Origami Flowers combines ancient yet simple origami techniques to create a wide variety of flowers. With step-by-step instructions for making over thirty flowers, the possibilities for origami floral arrangements are virtually endless. The ability to transform origami paper into hexagons, octagon, and other bases, then into beautiful flowers makes origami an inexpensive yet powerful crafting technique that you can start learning, creating, and experimenting with right now, then develop flowers of your own.

Fig. 1

NECESSARY ITEMS

ORIGAMI PAPERS

Origami papers must be sturdy enough to be folded repeatedly without tearing or ripping. Paper stores and craft stores sell origami paper. Origami papers are precut squares that have different-colored sides; one side is usually white. (See Fig. 1 and Fig. 2)

Fig. 2

Following are a few types of precut packaged origami papers:

- Textured (See Fig. 2 on page 10)
- Solid (See Fig. 3)
- Patterned (See Fig. 4)
- Double-sided with the same color

Fig. 3

Fig. 4

Any paper that can withstand repeated folding, such as gift wrap, computer paper, letterhead, and money, can be used to create these flowers. (See Fig. 5)

Fig. 5

When learning origami it is recommended that you start with large common origami paper. It is easier to learn folds on larger paper and visually easier to see the fold if the front and the back of the paper are different colors.

The choices of color and size of paper used contribute to the final outcome of the flower. The paper size and type of paper for each project have been included with the instructions. In several instances we have included a photo on the origami paper used before it was folded. For example, Starburst Dahlias on pages 90–92 use patterned paper with a yellow circle in the center. (See Fig. 6) After folding the paper as instructed, the flower stamen is created from the yellow center. (See Fig. 7) However, feel free to experiment with any desired colors, patterns, or paper size.

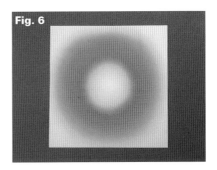
Fig. 6

Fig. 7

CUTTING TOOLS

There are various cutting tools that can be used to cut origami paper to size.

Rotary Trimmer

Rotary trimmers are great for cutting all types of paper stock and they work especially well with rolled paper as the pressure strip helps to keep the paper flat while cutting. (See Fig. 8) Some manufacturers offer interchangeable decorative-edged rotary blades that make patterned cuts that will add pizzazz to some of your origami creations. There is also a scoring blade that works well for scoring card stock and cover stock for heavier projects.

Hand-held Rotary Cutter

Hand-held rotary cutters will cut both paper and fabric. (See Fig. 9) You will need a cutting mat and a hard straightedge like a metal ruler to help hold down and trim the paper or fabric. If you will be using a rotary cutter for both fabric and paper, remember that fabric requires a sharp blade. Use older duller blades on paper to make the best use of the rotary blades. Blades for these cutters are also available in an assortment of decorative edges.

Scissors

Craft scissors are necessary for reducing large sheets or rolls of paper or fabric into more manageable sizes so that you can use rotary trimmers and cutters. (See Fig. 10) Scissors are also used for cutting nonstandard folding shapes. Smaller, sharp-pointed scissors are used for fine-detail cutting.

Decorative-edged Scissors

Decorative-edged scissors provide another way to make patterned cuts on the paper. (See See Fig. 10)

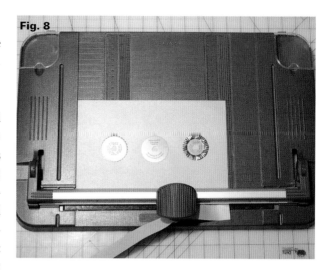

Fig. 8

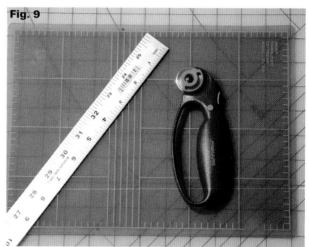

Fig. 9

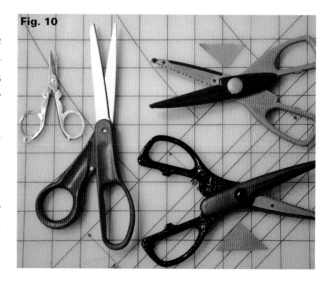

Fig. 10

MEASURING & SHAPING TOOLS

Measuring Sticks

Measuring sticks come in many lengths. Some are also flexible and can be used for tracing rounded curves on corners. Metal measuring sticks, also called straightedges, are not only useful for measuring but are essential when using a rotary cutter for safer, quicker, and cleaner paper cutting.

Fingers

Your fingers are essential for making sharp creases.

Scoring Blades & Bone Folders

Scoring blades and bone folders can be used to score precreases into heavy-paper stock. (See Fig. 11) Scoring blades are used with rotary trimmers to create a precrease. When using a bone folder to score heavy-paper stock, place a straightedge on the heavy-paper stock where the precrease is desired and slide the tip of the bone folder along the straightedge. To create a sharp precrease, lay the scored paper on a hard flat surface, make the fold, and slide the flat edge of the bone folder along the fold.

Pushing Tools

Long needles, wooden skewers, and opened paper clips are some examples of tools that are useful for gently pushing folded corners and points out. (See Fig. 11) These tools are useful when folding tiny pieces of origami.

GLUE

A glue stick is used for adhering petals in place and for mounting origami to other surfaces for decorative purposes.

FIXATIVES & SEALERS

Spray fixatives and sealers are used to preserve the surface of an origami project. (See Fig. 12) Spray acrylics and polyurethane glosses work to preserve and to stiffen origami creations made from paper. Always pretest the product to make certain that the spray will not destroy or warp the integrity of the material.

Fig. 11

Fig. 12

TERMS TO KNOW

Basic folds, basic forms

Basic folds are the common techniques used to make different base forms. Base Forms are on pages 20–29. An original origami project is the result of specific variations, or events, added onto one of these basic forms. Thus, several different origami projects can share the same base, which is made up of a common set of preliminary folds. Once you learn how to accomplish the basic forms, simply refer back to them before beginning a new project. The names given to these base forms may sometimes vary from one origami instructor to the next. Some instructors simply number their basic forms.

Crease, precrease

Sharp creases make a big difference in the final appearance of an origami model. Precreases are soft creases that make folding paper along a crease line easier to do.

Curling

Curling, or "to curl," refers to curling the origami model. This is usually done as one of the last steps when creating a flower. Curling can be done with the shaft of a ballpoint pen (See Fig. 13), the handle of craft knife, a wooden skewer, the edge of scissors (See Fig. 14), etc.

Fig. 13

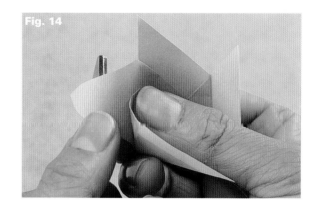

Fig. 14

Mountain Fold

This is a convex crease, or fold.

Score, scoring

A bone folder and straightedge or rotary scoring blades are used to lightly etch a crease line into a piece of heavy-paper stock in order to make a clean sharp precrease, or fold.

Valley Fold

This is a concave crease, or fold.

The following terms also have symbols to describe their actions:

- Crease, or Fold & Unfold on page 15
- Cut on page 15
- Fold Behind & Mountain Fold on page 15
- Fold in Front & Valley Fold on page 15
- Fold Over & Over on page 16
- Fold Over & Fold Back, or Pleat Fold on page 16
- Inflate on page 16
- Insert or Pull Out on page 16
- Inside Reverse Fold on page 17
- Outside Reverse Fold on page 17
- Place Finger Between Layers on page 17
- Press or Push In on page 17
- Previous Position on page 16
- Rotate the Model on page 16
- Turn Model Over on page 15

KEY FOR SYMBOLS

Symbols are used in origami to indicate a forthcoming action. In this book, the symbols will be placed on the photograph immediately before the text instructs the action.

Fold in Front & Valley Fold

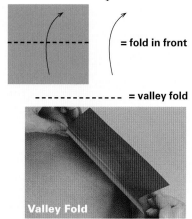

= fold in front

- - - - - - - - - - = valley fold

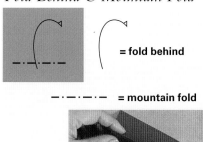

Valley Fold

Fold Behind & Mountain Fold

= fold behind

- · - · - · - = mountain fold

Mountain Fold

Cut

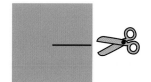

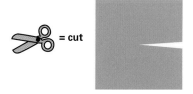

= cut

Crease, or Fold & Unfold

Turn Model Over

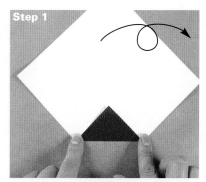

Step 1

Step 2

Fold Over & Over

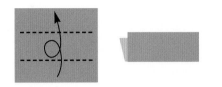

Step 1

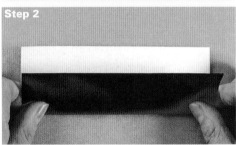

Step 2

Step 3

Rotate the Model

=
rotate the model

Inflate and Insert or Pull Out

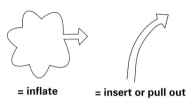

= inflate   = insert or pull out

Previous Position

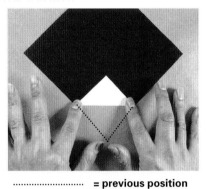

······················ = previous position

Fold Over & Fold Back, or Pleat Fold

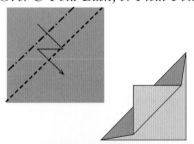

Step 1

Step 2

16

Press or Push In and Place Finger Between Layers

= press or push in **= place finger between layers**

Inside Reverse Fold

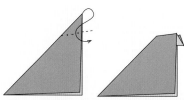

1. Crease tip.

2. Open model and collapse tip to inside.

3. Completed Inside Reverse Fold.

Outside Reverse Fold

1. Crease tip beyond the fold.

2. Crease tip to line up with the fold.

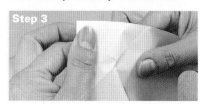

3. Open model.

4. Reverse fold to outside.

5. Pinch tip and pull it away from model to move fold to first crease line.

6. Completed Outside Reverse Fold.

17

MAKING A SHARP CREASE

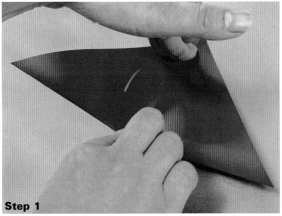

Step 1

1. Lay the paper on a hard flat surface. Make the indicated fold by matching up the points and holding them with the index finger of the left hand. Slide the index finger of the right hand from the matched points to the opposite side of the paper and the center of the fold.

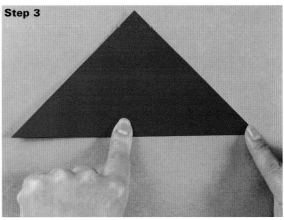

Step 3

3. Hold the center of the fold with the left-hand index finger and slide the right-hand index finger from the center of the fold outward to the right of the fold.

Step 2

2. Move the index finger on the left hand from the matched points and position it to the left of the right-hand index finger. Slide it from the center of the fold outward to the left along the fold.

FOLDING TIP

- When a flat surface is not available, you can also create a sharp crease by pinching the paper crease lightly between the thumbnail and index finger and moving along the edge of the fold. This method also comes in handy for relaxing an open crease or creating a light curl in the paper.

- Practice creasing until you are comfortable with the process and creating sharp creases.

BASIC FOLDS

Before learning a few common origami basic forms, practice simple convex and concave folding techniques to develop precision and crisp creasing.

Mountain and Valley Folds

Mountain and valley folds are also referred to as convex and concave folds. (See Fig. 15) The first fold—the convex, or mountain, fold (marked with a _._._._ line)—refers to folding down or away from you so that the crease faces toward you. The second fold—the concave, or valley, fold (marked with a _ _ _ _ line)—refers to folding up or toward you so that the crease faces away from you.

Accordion Folds

Accordion folds are also referred to as fan folds, shell folds, stair-step folds, and zigzag folds. These folds are simply consecutive convex and concave folds or pleats. (See Fig.16)

The top figure shows the accordion fold applied to a sheet of square paper and can be easily adapted to rectangular sheets.

The middle figure shows the accordion fold adapted to a circular piece of doily paper and can be easily applied to ovals and half circles.

The lower figure shows the accordion fold applied to a sheet of square paper folded along the diagonal and can be easily applied to triangles. This figure has been slightly gathered at the bottom to demonstrate how applying accordion folds to the diagonal of a square sheet can easily turn a square sheet into a leaf or frond.

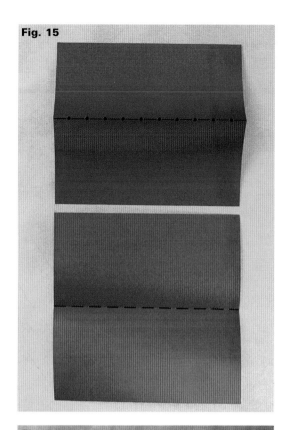

Fig. 15

Fig. 16

BASE FORMS

The following base forms are the foundations for creating every origami flower in this book. Once you have mastered these forms, you will be able to use them as a starting point and add onto them with specific folds to create a particular flower.

Ice Cream Base

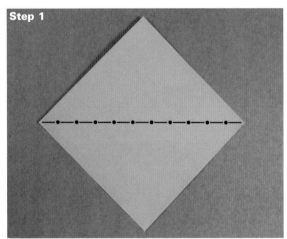

1. **Begin with a square.**

2. **Fold in half diagonally (wrong side of paper is on the inside).**

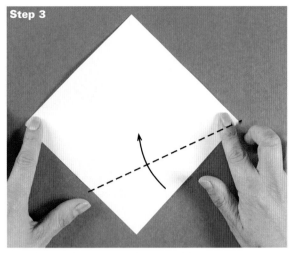

3. **Unfold to show crease. Turn model over.**

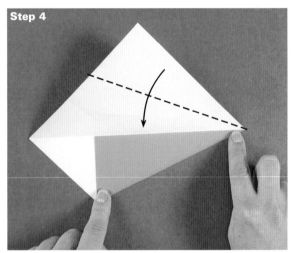

4. **Fold top and bottom right sides to the horizontal midline.**

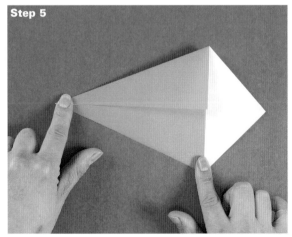

5. **Rotate model. Completed Ice Cream Base.**

Mat Base

Step 1

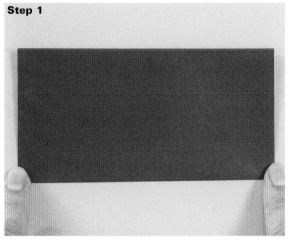

1. Begin with a square. Fold in half (wrong side of paper is inside).

Step 2

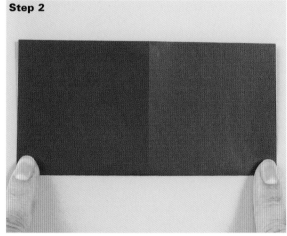

2. Unfold. Rotate and fold in half in the other direction.

Step 3

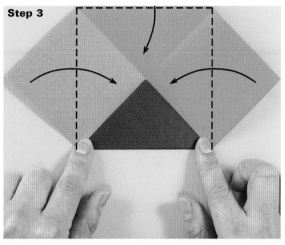

3. Unfold to show creases. Turn model over. Fold all corners to the center.

Step 4

4. Completed Mat Base.

Note: The Beautiful Blossoms on pages 64–65 begin with a mat base.

Square Pocket Base

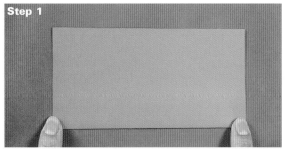

1. Begin with a square. Fold in half (wrong side of paper is inside).

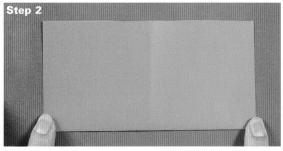

2. Unfold. Rotate and fold in half in other direction.

3. Unfold. Turn model over. Fold in half diagonally (right side of paper is inside).

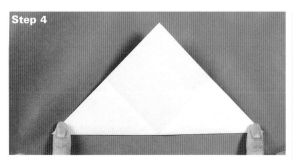

4. Unfold. Fold in half diagonally in other direction (right side of paper is inside).

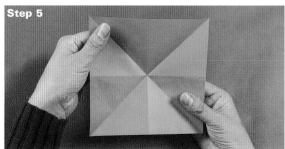

5. Unfold.

6. Fold two opposite side corners to meet at center.

7. Flatten model. Completed Square Pocket Base.

Note: The Enchanting Posies on pages 96–98 begin with a square pocket base.

22

Triangle Pocket Base

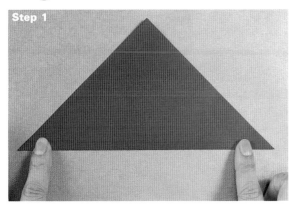

1. Begin with a square. Fold and unfold in half diagonally in both directions (wrong side of paper is inside).

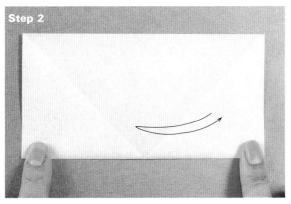

2. Turn model over. Rotate and fold in half (right side of paper is inside).

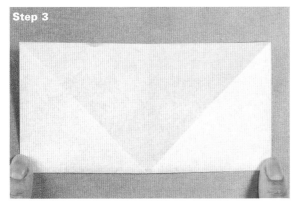

3. Unfold. Rotate and fold in half in other direction (right side of paper is inside).

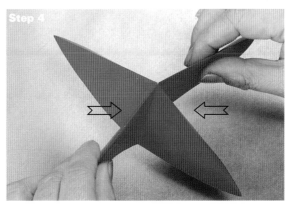

4. Unfold. Collapse two opposite sides to center along horizontal fold.

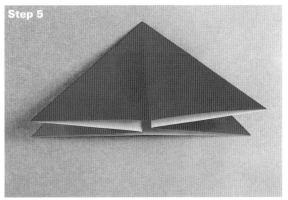

5. Flatten model. Completed Triangle Pocket Base.

Note: The Pretty Petals on pages 72–73 begin with a triangle pocket base.

Hexagon Base

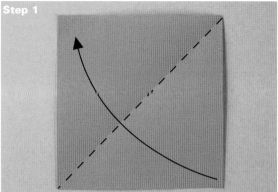

1. Fold in half diagonally (right side of paper is inside).

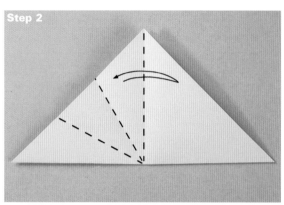

2. Fold left side into thirds. Unfold.

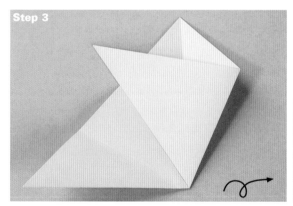

3. Match right side to two-thirds of left side.

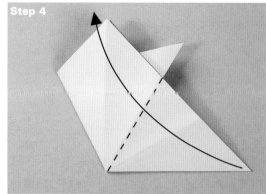

4. Turn model over. Fold right side as indicated.

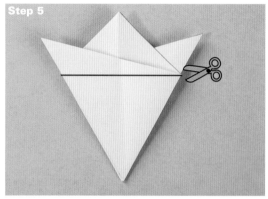

5. Cut off. Open.

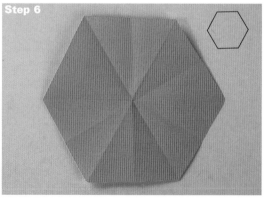

6. Completed Hexagon Base.

24

Octagon Base

Step 1

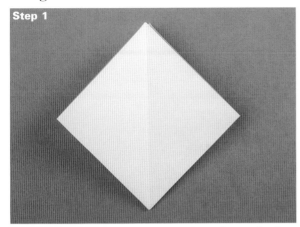

1. Begin with square pocket base. Refer to Square Pocket Base on page 22.

Step 2

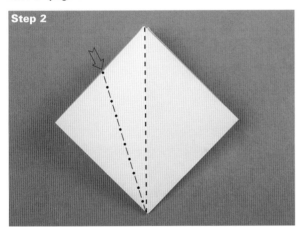

2. Fold top left flap to vertical midline. Unfold.

Step 3

3. Insert finger in pocket and move pocket over to vertical midline. Flatten.

Step 4

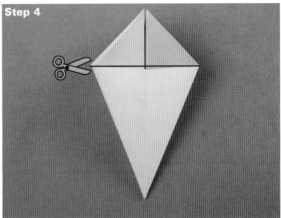

4. Repeat for remaining layers. Cut off top. Open.

Step 5

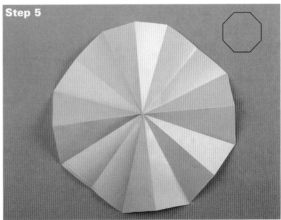

5. Completed Octagon Base.

Pentagon Base

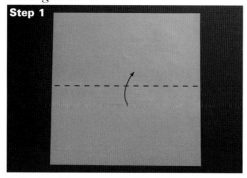

1. Begin with a square. Fold in half (right side of paper is inside).

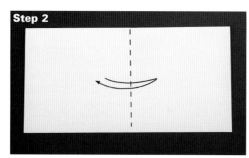

2. Fold in half again. Unfold once.

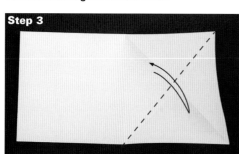

3. Fold bottom-right corner to vertical midline. Unfold.

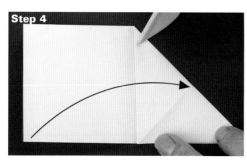

4. Fold top-right corner over to vertical midline. Bring bottom-left corner to center point of crisscross.

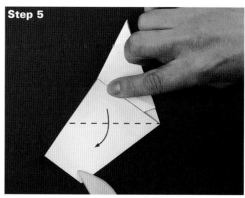

5. Crease. Fold down to bottom edge.

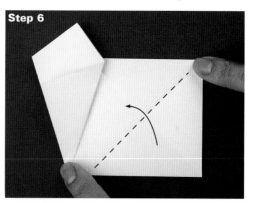

6. Rotate and open right side into a square.

7. Fold bottom-right corner to top edge.

Step 8

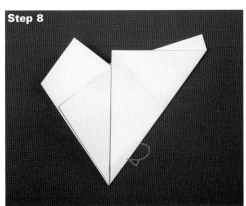

8. **Turn model over. Fold as shown.**

Step 9

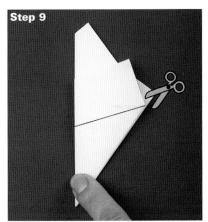

9. **Turn model over and cut off top as indicated.**

Step 10

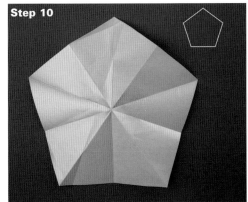

10. **Completed Pentagon Base.**

Note: **The Blooming Starfish on pages 99–101 begins with a pentagon base.**

Long Triangle Base

Step 1

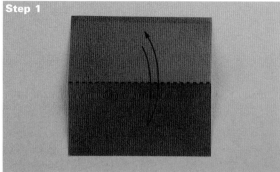

1. Fold in half. Unfold.

Step 2

2. Fold bottom right-corner up to horizontal midline. Unfold.

Step 3

3. Fold bottom left-corner up to horizontal midline. Unfold.

Step 4

4. Cut as indicated.

Step 5

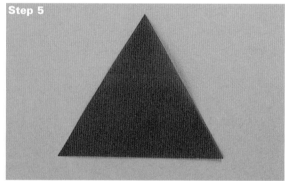

5. Completed Long Triangle.

FOLDING TIPS

- Follow all steps in order. After each fold, position your model exactly as shown in the photograph.

- Be aware of the progression of the form—keep in mind the previous step and be prepared for the next.

- Study the form.

- Make accurate cuts.

- Use your imagination.

- Have fun.

Triangle Base

Step 1

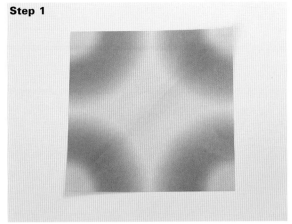

1. Begin with a square.

Step 2

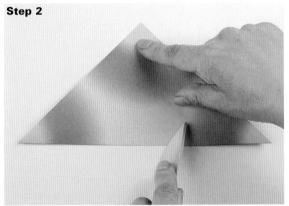

2. Fold square in half, creating a triangle. Unfold.

Step 3

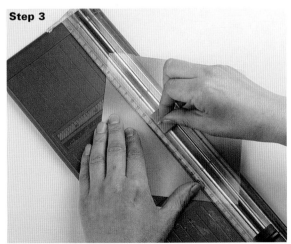

3. Cut on crease.

Step 4

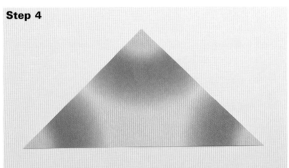

4. Completed Triangle Base.

FOLDING TIPS

- Dedicate a time and place for origami as it requires a high level of concentration.

- Whenever possible, work on a hard flat surface.

- Use a paper that is thin yet strong enough to withstand continuous folding without stretching.

- Work with precision and exactness, making straight folds and clean corners.

- Smooth all folds and creases with your thumbnail, a library or credit card, or a bone folder.

- Read all instructions carefully.

- Begin by using origami paper that is colored differently on each side so you can tell the front from the back.

BLOOMING PETALS

GIVING THANKS

NECESSARY ITEMS:

- Origami paper: 1" circle, patterned (10)
- Glue stick

NECESSARY FOLDS:

Step 4

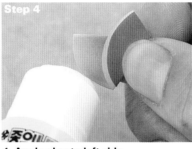

4. Apply glue to left side.

Step 6

6. Completed Giving Thanks.

Step 1

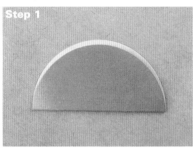

1. Fold circle almost horizontally in half (wrong side of paper is inside).

Step 5a

Step 5b

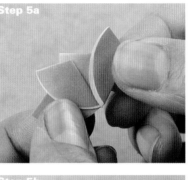

Step 2

2. Turn model over. Fold almost in half.

Step 3

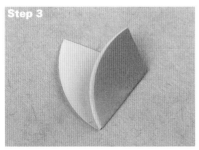

3. Repeat nine times for a total of ten petals.

Step 5c

5. Glue petals together.

Note: Craft stamens have been adhered to the centers of these flowers.

33

NECESSARY ITEMS:

- Origami paper: 2", patterned (8)
- Curling tool
- Glue stick

NECESSARY FOLDS:

Step 1

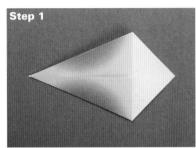

1. Begin with ice cream base. Refer to Ice Cream Base on page 20. Turn model over.

Step 2

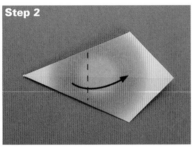

2. Fold bottom to horizontal midline.

Step 3

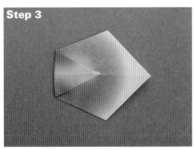

3. Repeat Steps 1–2 seven times for a total of eight petals.

Step 4

4. Place glue on back side of bottom left corner.

Step 5a

Step 5b

Step 5c

5. Glue petals together.

Step 6

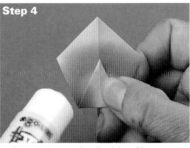

6. Curl petals.

Step 7

7. Complete poppy.

Note: Dried seeds have been added to the poppy center for the stamen.

PURPLE STARS

NECESSARY ITEMS:

- Origami paper: 2", patterned (5)
- Glue stick

NECESSARY FOLDS:

Step 1

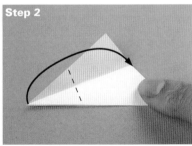

1. Begin with ice cream base. Refer to Ice Cream Base on page 20. Fold in half, backward.

Step 2

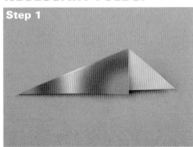

2. Unfold top flap.

Step 3

3. Fold left side to right edge.

Step 4

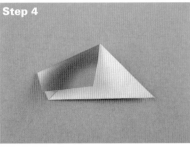

4. Fold top down.

5. Repeat Steps 1–4 four times for a total of five petals.

Step 6

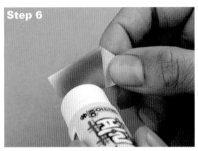

6. Apply glue to petals. Glue petals together.

Step 7

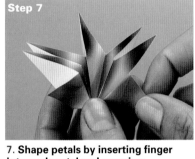

7. Shape petals by inserting finger into each petal and pressing toward tip.

Step 8

8. Completed Purple Star.

Note: Craft stamens have been inserted down through the centers of these Purple Stars.

PERFECT PEONIES

Developed by Soonboke Smith

NECESSARY ITEMS:

- Origami paper: 4" patterned (5)
- Curling tool
- Glue stick

NECESSARY FOLDS:

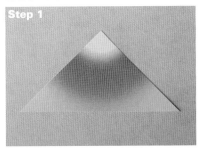

1. Begin with a triangle base. Refer to Triangle Base on page 29.

2. Turn model over.

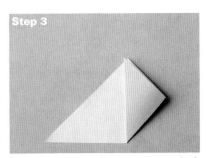

3. Fold bottom-right corner to vertical midline.

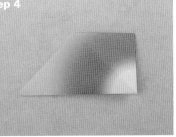

4. Turn model over.

5. Repeat Steps 1–4 four times for a total of five petals.

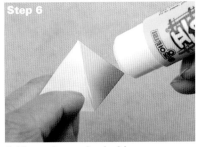

6. Place glue on back side.

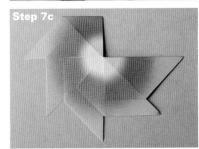

7. Glue petals together.

PERFECT PEONIES CONTINUED ▶

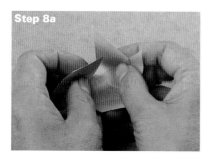

Step 8a

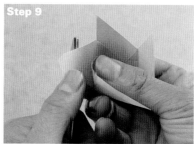

Step 9

9. **Curl petals.**

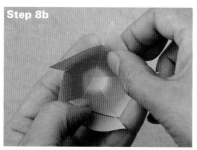

Step 8b

8. **Shape petals.**

Step 10

10. **Completed peony.**

Notes: A craft stamen has been adhered to the center of the flower. Place several peonies together for a peony cluster.

Note: The flowers above are made from solid-colored origami paper and silk craft pistils have been inserted down through the center. They were created based on the Perfect Peonies on pages 38–40.

NECESSARY ITEMS:

- Origami paper: 1½", patterned (8)
- Glue stick
- Small craft scissors

NECESSARY FOLDS:

1. Begin with mat base. Refer to Mat Base on page 21. Unfold bottom flaps.

2. Fold bottom-left and bottom-right corners back to vertical midline.

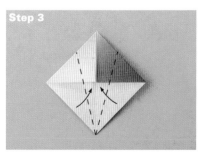

3. Fold left and right side to vertical midline. Unfold left and right side from back.

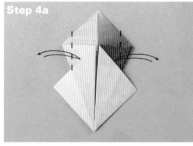

4. Fold top-left and top-right corners as indicated. Unfold.

5. Insert finger into right pocket. Push in and crease remaining paper under top right side of middle flap. Repeat for left side pocket.

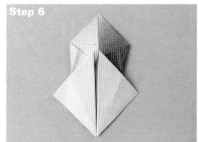

6. Turn model over.

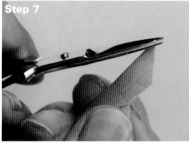

7. Fold top almost vertically in half. Using small craft scissors, cut a "V" shape in petal tip.

8. Repeat Steps 1–7 seven times for a total of eight petals.

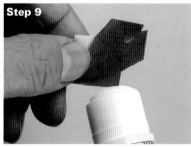

9. Apply glue to right petal flap.

43

CRAZY COSMOS CONTINUED ▶

Step 10a

Step 10b

Step 10c

10. Glue petals together.

Step 11

11. Completed cosmo.

Note: Craft stamens have been inserted down through the centers of these cosmos.

STAR FLOWER

STAR FLOWER

Developed by Soonboke Smith

NECESSARY ITEMS:

- Origami paper: 2", patterned (5)
- Glue stick

NECESSARY FOLDS:

Step 1

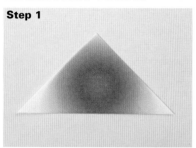

1. Begin with triangle base. Refer to Triangle base on page 29. Turn model over. Fold in half, matching right side to left side. Unfold.

Step 2

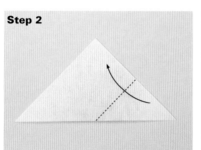

2. Fold bottom-right corner up to vertical midline.

Step 3

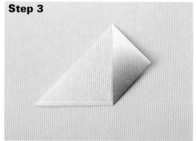

3. Fold bottom-left corner up to vertical midline.

Step 4

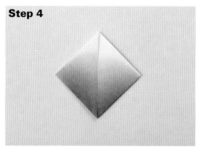

4. Fold bottom-left corner up to vertical midline. Glue to secure.

5. Repeat Steps 1–5 four times for a total of five petals.

Step 6

6. Turn model over. Apply glue onto petal edge.

Step 7a

Step 7b

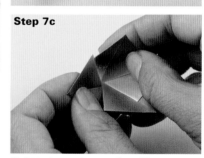

Step 7c

7. Attach petals together. Shape flower.

Step 8

8. Completed Star Flower.

PINWHEEL DAISIES

PINWHEEL DAISIES

NECESSARY ITEMS:

- Origami paper: 3", patterned (4)
- Glue stick

NECESSARY FOLDS:

Step 1

1. Begin with mat base. Refer to Mat Base on page 21.

Step 2

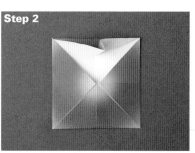

2. Fold bottom-left corner of the top triangle up to crease line. Unfold. Repeat for bottom-right corner of top triangle. Unfold. Push up right side. Push up left side, overlapping right.

Step 3

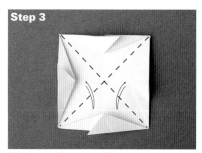

3. Repeat Steps 2–3 for each triangle.

4. Fold and unfold both sides diagonally.

Step 5a

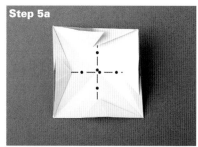

Step 5b

5. Fold in half in both directions.

Step 6

6. Hold as shown and collapse.

Step 7

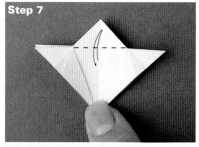

7. Fold tip down and unfold to crease.

Step 8

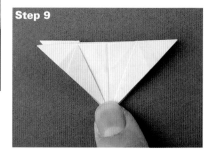

8. Open. Insert fingers between layers. With center star facing up, fold each side in and under, collapsing the center star.

Step 9

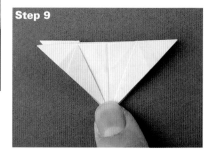

9. Flatten.

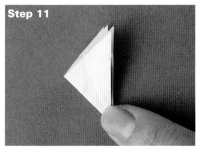

Step 11

11. Fold in half, at center vertical creases.

12. Repeat Steps 1–11 three times for a total of four petals

Step 13

13. Apply glue to petal as shown.

Step 14a

Step 14b

14. Attach petals.

Step 15

15. Open flower and shape petals.

Step 16

16. Turn model over and press between each tip.

Step 17

17. Completed Pinwheel daisy.

Note: Pinwheel Daisy close-up front view.

Note: Pinwheel Daisy close-up back view.

49

NECESSARY ITEMS:

- Origami paper: 3", 2", 1", textured (2)
- Floral stem wire
- Glue stick
- Green floral tape
- Paper towel strip

NECESSARY FOLDS:

1. Begin with square pocket base. Refer to Square Pocket Base on page 22.

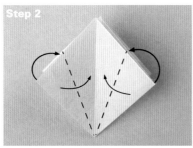

2. Fold left and right bottom sides to vertical midline. Turn model over. Repeat.

5. Using small craft scissors, cut slits on every other crease as indicated.

8. Open.

9. Repeat Steps 1–6 four times for one carnation.

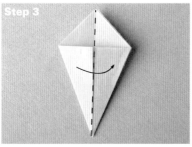

3. Fold in half vertically.

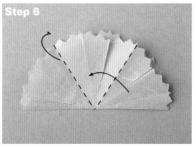

6. Fold in half. <u>Do not align slits.</u>

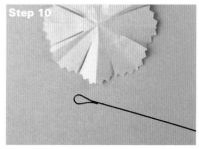

10. Create a small loop at one end of wire.

4. Using pinking edge scissors, cut off tip slightly below the midline.

7. Fold left side to vertical midline. Fold right side to vertical midline. Twist ends two or three times.

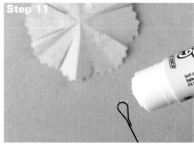

11. Cover loop with glue.

50

SWEET CARNATIONS CONTINUED ▶

SWEET CARNATIONS

12. Insert nonloop end of wire through bottom center of carnation petals.

Note: Insert wire through largest petal first, medium-sized petal second, then smaller petals.

13. Wrap a narrow strip of paper towel at base of carnation.

14. Cover paper strip and wire with green floral tape.

52

Step 15

15. Completed carnation.

Note: Close-up of the Sweet Carnations.

FLOWER FIREWORKS

FLOWER FIREWORKS

Developed by Soonboke Smith

NECESSARY ITEMS:

- Origami paper: 3", patterned
- Glue stick
- Small craft scissors

NECESSARY FOLDS:

1. Begin with square pocket base. Refer to Square Pocket Base on page 22.

Step 2

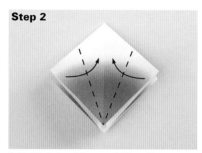

2. Fold right side to midline. Repeat for left side.

Step 3

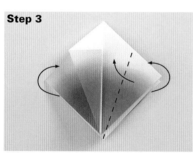

3. Turn model over. Repeat Step 2.

Step 4a

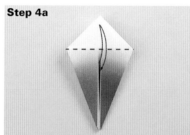

Step 4b

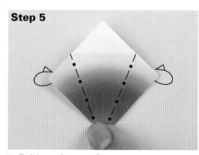

4. Fold tip down. Unfold.

Step 5

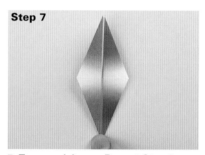

5. Fold as shown. Open.

Step 6

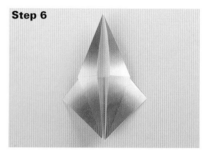

6. Insert finger between layers. Lift and flatten.

Step 7

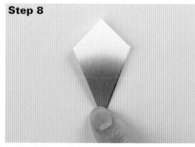

7. Turn model over. Repeat Step 6.

Step 8

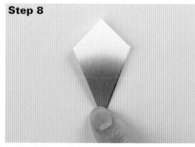

8. Fold flaps down.

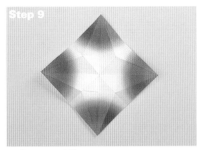

9. Open and flatten.

14. Apply glue to petal as shown.

17. Using craft scissors, diagonally cut off each petal tip.

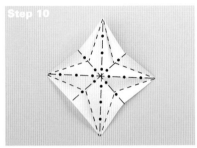

10. Turn model over. Fold as shown.

15. Glue petals together.

18. Completed Flower Fireworks.

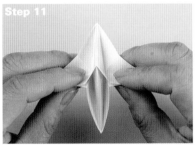

11. Push together as shown.

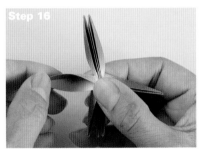

16. Insert fingers into petals. Shape.

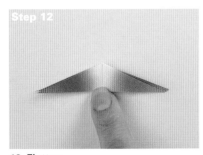

12. Flatten.

13. Repeat Steps 1–12 one time for two petals.

Note: Close-up of the Flower Fireworks.

CUTE CLOVERS

NECESSARY ITEMS:

- Origami paper: 3", patterned
- Glue stick
- Small craft scissors

NECESSARY FOLDS:

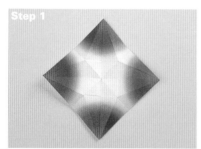

1. Follow Flower Fireworks
Steps 1–15 on pages 54–55.

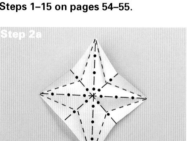

2. Insert finger into pocket and shape petal. Repeat for remaining petals.

3. Glue tip in back to secure.

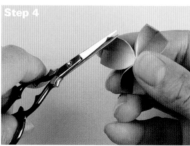

4. Using small craft scissors, diagonally cut off the corner of each petal.

5. Completed clover.

Note: **Close-up of the Cute Clovers.**

BLOOMING FLOWERS

ELEGANT IRISES

NECESSARY ITEMS:

- Origami paper: 3", solid
- Curling tool
- Glue stick

NECESSARY FOLDS:

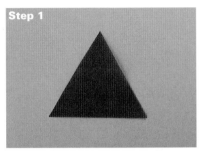

1. Begin with long triangle. Refer to Long Triangle base on page 28. Turn model over.

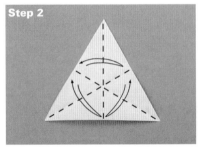

2. Fold in half, lengthwise. Unfold. Rotate. Fold in half, lengthwise. Unfold. Rotate. Fold in half, lengthwise. Rotate.

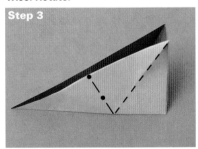

3. Insert finger into right pocket. Move pocket to vertical midline.

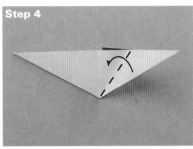

4. Fold right side to midline. Unfold. Insert finger into pocket and move pocket to center.

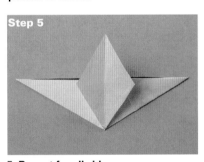

5. Repeat for all sides.

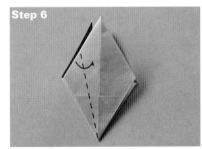

6. Fold right and left sides to vertical midline. Glue.

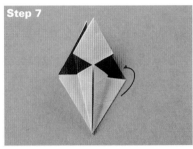

7. Turn model over. Repeat Step 6.

8. Turn model over. Repeat Step 6. Glue.

61

ELEGANT IRISES CONTINUED ▶

9. Curl petals.

10. Completed iris.

Note: A craft stamen has been inserted down through the center of each iris.

LOVELY LILIES

NECESSARY ITEMS:

- Origami paper: 6", solid (2)
- Glue stick
- Curling tool

NECESSARY FOLDS:

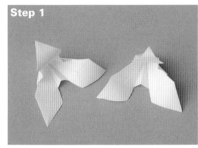

Step 1

1. Refer to Elegant Irises on pages 61–62. Make two irises.

Step 2

2. Apply glue to bottom back side of one iris. Insert iris with glue into remaining iris, alternating petals.

Step 3

3. Press top petals to secure. Completed lily.

Note: Craft stamens have been inserted down through the centers of these lilies.

BEAUTIFUL BLOSSOMS

NECESSARY ITEMS:

- Origami paper: 3", patterned
- Curling tool

NECESSARY FOLDS:

1. Begin with mat base. Refer to Mat Base on page 21.

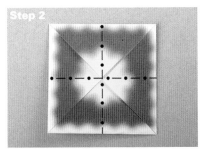

2. Fold and unfold as shown.

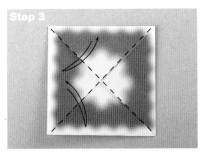

3. Turn model over. Fold and unfold as shown.

4. Collapse into square pocket base.

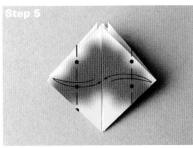

5. Fold top layer as shown. Unfold. Turn model over. Repeat.

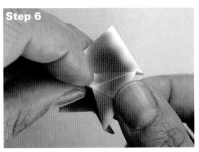

6. Insert finger into right pocket. Make inside reverse fold. Repeat for left pocket.

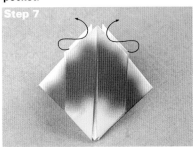

7. Turn model over. Repeat Steps 6–7.

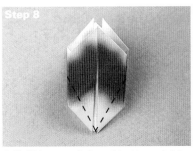

8. Fold bottom-left and bottom-right corners to vertical midline.

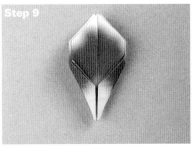

9. Turn model over. Repeat Step 7.

10. Open flower by pulling downward on petal. Curl.

11. Completed Beautiful Blossom.

NECESSARY ITEMS:

- Origami paper: 6", patterned
- Curling tool

NECESSARY FOLDS:

1. Begin with mat base. Refer to Mat Base on page 21.

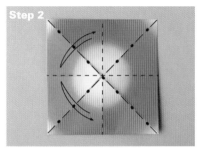

Step 2

2. Fold in half. Unfold. Rotate model and repeat in opposite direction. Turn model over. Fold in half, diagonally. Unfold. Rotate model. Repeat. Collapse mat base into square pocket base.

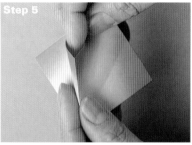

Step 5

5. Pinch bottom and top of pocket.

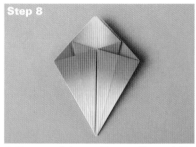

Step 8

8. Turn model over. Repeat Steps 4–7.

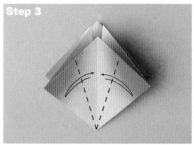

Step 3

3. Fold left side slightly past vertical midline. Fold bottom-right side over left fold (in thirds). Unfold. Turn model over. Repeat.

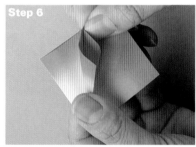

Step 6

6. Move pocket to left.

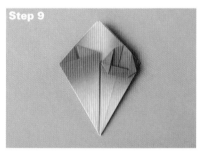

Step 9

9. Fold right pocket opening down, push sides in, and flatten.

10. Repeat Step 9 on left side.

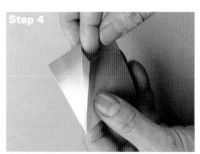

Step 4

4. Insert finger in left pocket as shown.

Step 7

7. Repeat Steps 4–6 for right side, moving the pocket to the right.

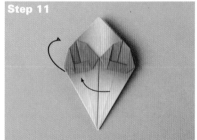

Step 11

11. Fold right side over left side. Fold left backside over to right side.

CHARMING ANEMONIES CONTINUED ▶

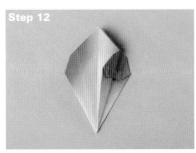

12. Fold right side in half. Repeat for left side.

15. Open flower by pulling petals downward. Curl petals.

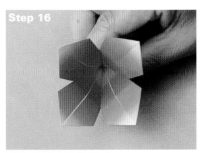

16. Completed anemone.

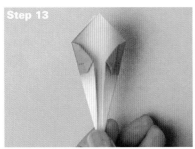

13. Turn model over. Repeat Step 12.

14. Hold opposite sides of model as shown.

Note: Craft stamens have been inserted down through the centers of these anemonies.

COLOR SPOTS

COLOR SPOTS

NECESSARY ITEMS:

- Origami paper: 2", patterned

NECESSARY FOLDS:

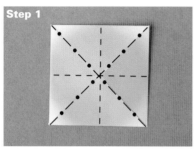

Step 1

1. Begin with mat base. Refer to Mat Base on page 21.

Step 2

2. Fold in half. Unfold. Rotate model. Repeat.

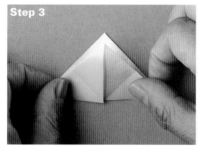

Step 3

3. Fold in half diagonally. Unfold. Rotate model. Repeat.

Step 4

4. Collapse the model into square pocket base.

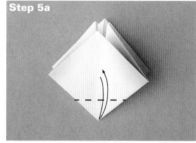

Step 5a

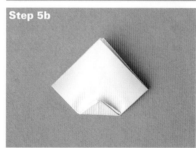

Step 5b

5. Fold bottom up, just below midpoint. Unfold.

Step 6

6. Open to beginning mat base.

Step 7

7. With the center square facing up, fold each side in and under, collapsing the center square. Flatten model.

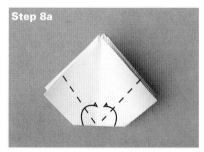
Step 8a

Step 10

10. Fold corner of right pocket down. Press edges. Repeat for left side.

Step 13

13. Completed Color Spot.

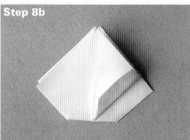
Step 8b

8. Fold bottom sides to vertical midline. Turn model over. Repeat.

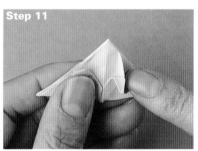
Step 11

11. Turn model over. Repeat for each side.

Step 9a

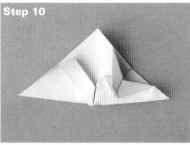
Step 12

12. Open flower by puling petals downward.

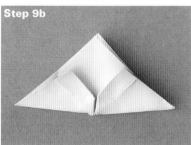
Step 9b

9. Insert finger between layers and open. Repeat for other side.

Note: Close-up of Color Spots.

NECESSARY ITEMS:

- Origami paper: 3", patterned
- Bead
- Glue stick

NECESSARY FOLDS:

1. Begin with triangle pocket base. Refer to Triangle Pocket Base on page 23.

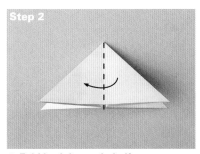

2. Fold both layers in half.

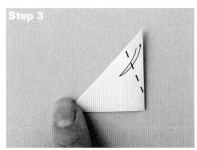

3. Fold top down and to the left as shown. Unfold.

Step 4a

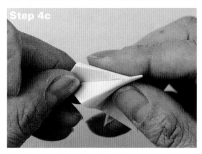

Step 4b

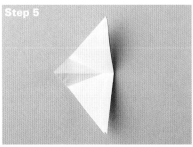

Step 4c

4. Open and make inside reverse fold.

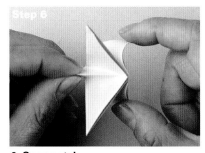

Step 5

5. Pinch tip.

6. Open petals.

Step 7a

Step 7b

7. Shape petals by inserting finger and pressing out the tips. Do not let go of the pinched tip.

Step 9

8. Glue bead to center. Completed Pretty Petal.

SPRING TULIPS

NECESSARY ITEMS:

- Origami paper: 3", solid for tulip head; 6", solid for tulip stem
- Stem wire

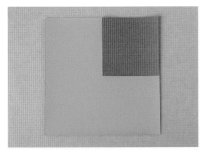

Note: Notice the size difference between the paper used for the tulip head and the paper used for the tulip stem.

NECESSARY FOLDS:

1. Begin with square pocket base. Refer to Square Pocket Base on page 22.

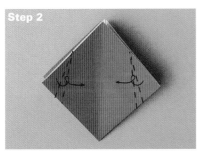

2. Fold and roll top layer of left side. Repeat for far side. Turn model over and repeat.

3. Fold bottom up. Unfold.

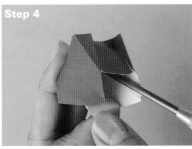

4. Open flower. Using a pointed object, make a small hole in tulip bottom. Flatten tulip base.

5. Shape petals by pulling downward.

6. Completed tulip head.

NECESSARY FOLDS

FOR TULIP STEM:

Note: The tulip stems are not featured in the photograph on page 74.

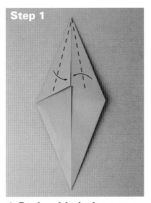

1. Begin with the ice cream base. Refer to Ice Cream Base on page 20. Fold top-corners to the horizontal midline.

2. Repeat.

SPRING TULIPS CONTINUED ▶

Step 3a

Step 3b

Step 3c

3. Rotate. Fold as shown.

Step 4

4. Pull out center.

ASSEMBLING TULIP:

Step 1

1. Insert stem into bottom of tulip head.

Step 2

2. Completed tulip.

Note: Craft stamens have been inserted down through the centers of these tulips.

DELICATE BELLFLOWERS

DELICATE BELLFLOWERS

NECESSARY ITEMS:

- Origami paper: 3", solid
- Craft stamen with wire stem
- Glue stick

NECESSARY FOLDS:

1. Begin with the square pocket base. Refer to the Square Pocket Base on page 22.

Step 2

2. Fold top-left corner and bottom right-corner to diagonal midline. Unfold.

Step 3

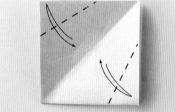

3. Turn model over. Repeat.

Step 4a

Step 4b

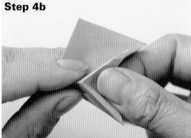

4. Insert finger into right side pocket. Make inside reverse fold.

Step 5

5. Repeat for each pocket.

Step 6

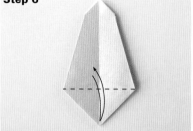

6. Fold bottom tip up as shown. Unfold.

Step 7

7. Apply glue to inside of petals on the inside reverse fold. Allow to dry.

Step 8

8. Insert craft stamen down through the center of the bellflower.

Step 9

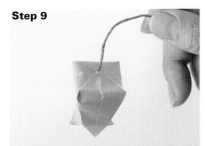

9. Open flower by pulling petal tips downward and pushing up base to flatten.

Step 10

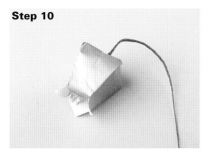

10. Completed Bellflower.

Note: Close-up of Delicate Bellflowers.

VIVID VIOLETS

NECESSARY ITEMS:

- Origami paper: 3", patterned
- Small craft scissors

NECESSARY FOLDS:

1. Begin with the square pocket base. Refer to the Square Pocket Base on page 22.

Step 5a

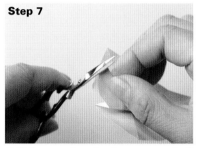

Step 2

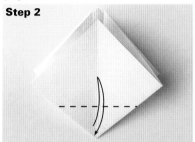

2. With opening at the top of the model, fold bottom up to midpoint. Unfold.

Step 5b

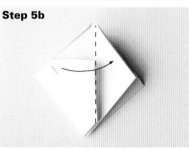

5. Fold bottom-left corner to slightly past midline. Repeat for other side, folding to midline, not overlapping.

Step 7

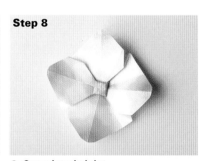

7. Using small craft scissors, round off each petal tip.

Step 3

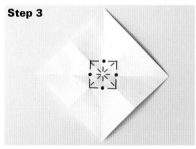

3. Open. With center square facing up, fold each side in and under, collapsing the center square. Flatten model. Refer to Color Spots on pages 69–71.

Step 6a

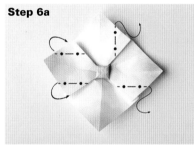

Step 6b

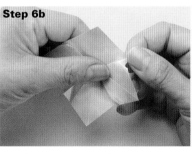

Step 8

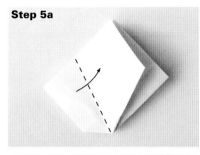

8. Completed violet.

Step 4

4. Fold bottom-right side to midline. Fold bottom-left side to slightly overlap midline. Fold top layer in half along midline. Fold bottom-left side slightly past midline. Turn model over. Fold bottom-left side to midline. Fold top layer in half along midline. Turn model over.

Step 6c

6. Open flower. Fold sides as shown. Unfold. Make inside reverse folds.

Note: Close-up of Vivid Violets.

MORNING GLORIES

NECESSARY ITEMS:

- Origami paper: 3", patterned
- Glue stick

NECESSARY FOLDS:

1. Begin with the square pocket base. Refer to the Square Pocket Base on page 22.

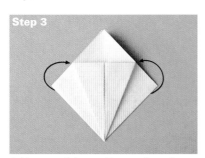

2. Fold right side to vertical midline. Repeat for left side.

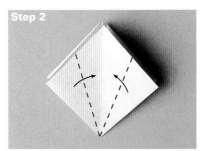

3. Turn model over. Repeat Step 2.

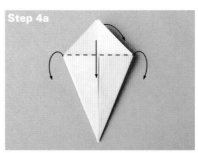

4a.

4b.

4. Fold tip down. Repeat for each tip.

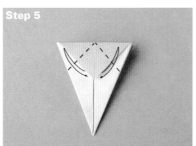

5. Fold right tip down to crease line. Repeat for left side. Turn model over. Repeat for each side. Unfold.

6. Open each tip and apply glue to underside. Press tips down.

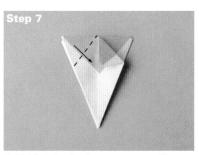

7. Fold right tip down to crease line. Repeat for opposite side.

8. Turn the model over. Repeat for both sides.

MORNING GLORIES CONTINUED ▶

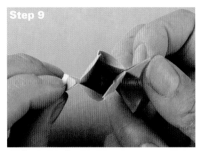

9. Open as shown.

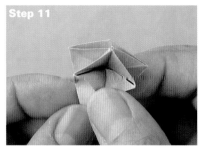

11. Insert finger into pocket and fold sides down as shown.

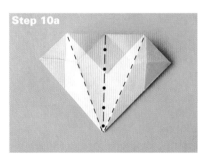

12. Open flower by pulling petals downward. Shape flower.

10. Flatten and fold as shown. Pinch corners and push together to collapse.

13. Completed Morning Glory.

Note: Craft stamens have been inserted down through the centers of these Morning Glories.

PERIWINKLE PATCH

PERIWINKLE PATCH

NECESSARY ITEMS:

- Origami paper: 2", patterned
- Glue stick
- Pinking edged scissors

NECESSARY FOLDS:

1. Begin with the square pocket base. Refer to the Square Pocket Base on page 22.

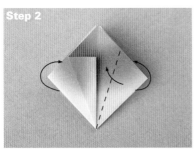

2. Fold right and left sides to midline.

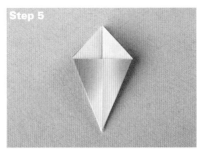

5. Repeat for remaining layers.

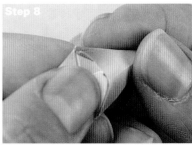

8. Turn model over and repeat for opposite side.

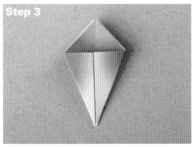

3. Turn model over. Repeat Step 2.

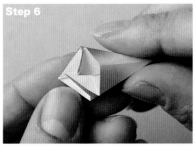

6. Open pocket.

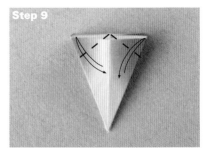

9. Rotate model.

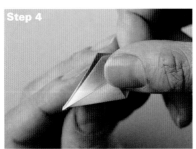

4. Insert finger into pocket and move pocket to midline.

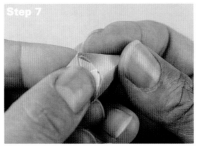

7. Tuck tip inside.

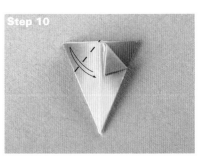

10. Fold top-right corner to midline. Repeat for top left corner. Unfold.

Note: Close-up of Periwinkle Patch.

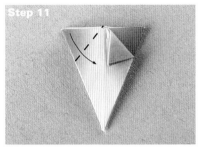

11. Turn model over. Repeat Step 9.

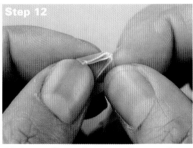

12. Insert finger between layers of bottom-left side pocket and move pocket to midline.

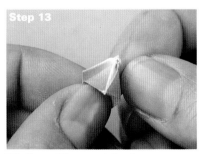

13. Repeat for remaining layers.

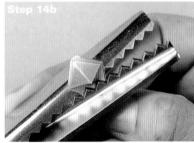

14. Using pinking-edged scissors, cut off bottom as indicated.

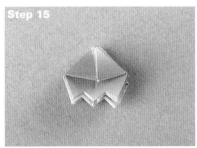

15. Rotate model and grab opposite sides. Open all four pockets.

16. Insert fingers and thumb into pockets. Open out like a fan.

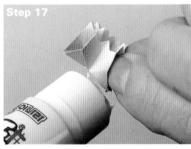

17. Turn model over. Glue center together as shown.

18. Completed Periwinkle Patch.

87

88

Note: This is the Periwinkle Patch, on pages 85–87, folded with a different color of paper.

PERIWINKLE ADAPTATION

NECESSARY ITEMS:

- Origami paper: 3", solid

NECESSARY FOLDS:

1. Begin with the square pocket base with color on inside. Refer to the Square Pocket Base on page 22.

2. Follow Periwinkle Patch Steps 2–5 on page 86. Fold top-right layer to left side along midline. Fold top of cone down along midline. Repeat for remaining sides.

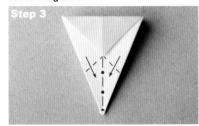

3. Fold as shown. Fold all layers together.

4. Pinch.

5. Open flower and shape petals by pressing down.

6. Completed periwinkle adaptation.

STARBURST DAHLIAS

Developed by Soonboke Smith

NECESSARY ITEMS:

- Origami paper: 6" solid
- Small craft scissors

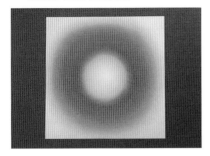

NECESSARY FOLDS:

1. Begin with the square pocket base. Refer to the Square Pocket Base on page 22.

2. Fold lower left side to midline. Repeat for right side. Turn model over. Repeat. Insert finger into pocket and move pocket to midline. Repeat for remain-ing layers. Fold tip down to mid-line. Repeat for remaining layers.

Step 3

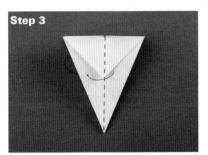

3. Fold left side over to right side. Turn model over. Repeat.

Step 4

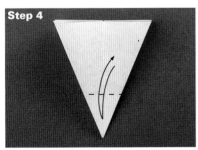

4. Fold bottom tip up ⅜" from top edge. Unfold.

Step 5

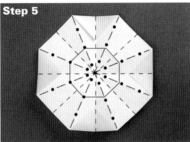

5. Open.

Step 6a

Step 6b

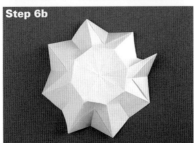

6. Fold on creases as shown.

Step 7

7. Fold as shown to flatten.

Step 8

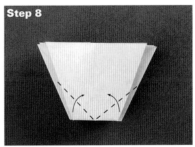

8. Fold bottom-left and right corners to midline. Repeat for each layer. Make certain layer does not have a folded down tip from Step 2.

91

STARBURST DAHLIAS CONTINUED ▶

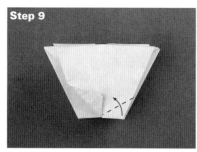

Step 9

9. Fold bottom-right corners to midline. Repeat for each layer.

Step 10

10. Fold edge of each petal center down to middle, while pinching sides.

Step 11

11. Using small craft scissors, diagonally cut off each petal tip.

Step 12

12. Shape petals from underneath.

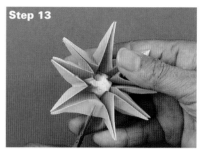

Step 13

13. Cut small slits in between each petal. Shape.

Step 14

14. Completed Stardust Dahlia.

Note: Close-up of Starburst Dahlias.

92

NECESSARY ITEMS:

- Origami paper: 3", patterned

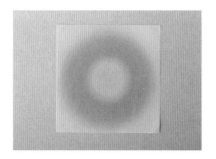

NECESSARY FOLDS:

1. Begin with the square pocket base. Refer to the Square Pocket Base on page 22.

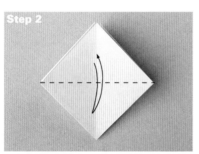

2. Fold in half, matching tips. Unfold.

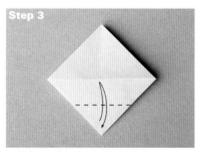

3. Fold and unfold where indicated by dashed line.

4. Open.

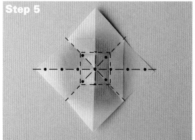

5. Flatten and fold as shown.

Note: Make certain creases are very crisp.

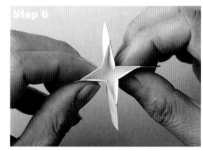

6. With center square facing up, collapse each side in and under. Flatten.

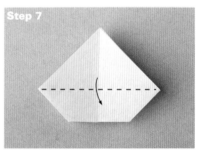

7. Fold as indicated.

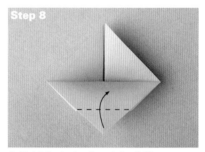

8. Fold tip to horizontal midline.

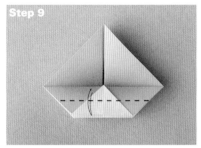

Step 9

9. Fold bottom tip to horizontal midline. Unfold.

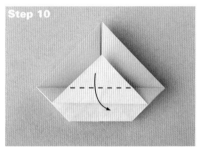

Step 10

10. Fold tip up as shown.

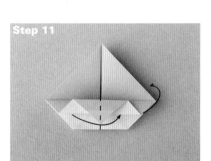

Step 11

11. Fold tip down as shown. Fold top-left layer in direction of arrow. Fold bottom-right layer back in direction of arrow.

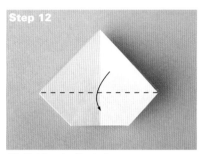

Step 12

12. Fold as indicated.

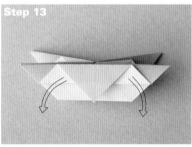

Step 13

13. Repeat Steps 7–12 for remaining layers.

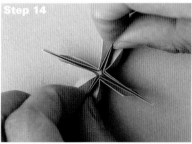

Step 14

14. Holding opposite sides of model, insert fingers into layers as shown. Shape.

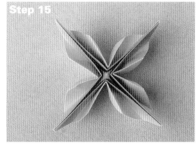

Step 15

15. Completed Orange Twinkle.

Note: Close-up of Orange Twinkles.

NECESSARY ITEMS:

* Origami paper: 6", patterned

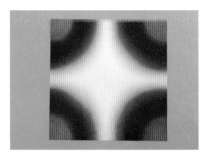

NECESSARY FOLDS:

1. Begin with the square pocket base. Refer to the Square Pocket Base on page 22.

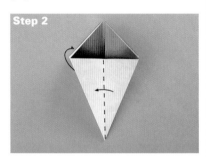

Step 2

2. Fold right and left sides to midline. Turn model over. Repeat. Open left side. Insert finger into pocket. Move to midline. Repeat for remaining layers.

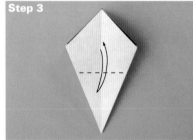

Step 3

3. Fold in half. Unfold.

Step 4

4. Insert finger into pocket.

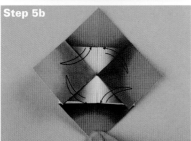

Step 5a

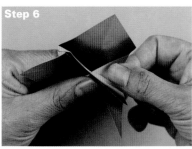

Step 5b

5. Pull tips down and flatten model.

Step 6

6. Insert finger into pocket and make inside reverse fold. Repeat for each pocket.

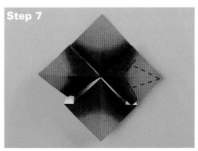

Step 7

7. Fold top and bottom sides of right petal to horizontal midline. Repeat for opposite petals.

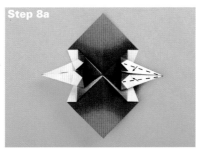

Step 8a

Step 8b

8. Once again, fold top and bottom sides of right petal to horizontal midline. Repeat for opposite petal.

Note: The folds made in Steps 7–8 are used to create "texture" on the petals.

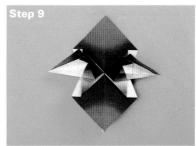

Step 9

9. Open petals.

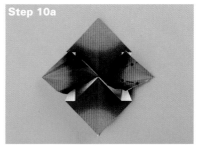

Step 10a

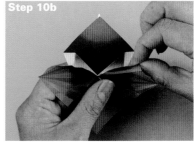

Step 10b

10. Fold sides as shown. Repeat for opposite petal.

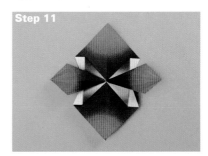

Step 11

11. Glue petal flaps on underside. Let dry. Turn model over and rotate.

97

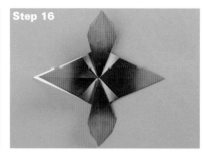

Step 12

12. Fold top and bottom corners to center line.

Step 16

16. Turn model over. Slightly fold under the sides of the textured petals to round the edges. Completed Enchanting Posies.

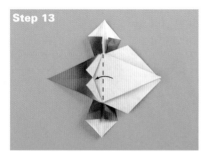

Step 13

13. Fold right tip over to left tip.

Step 14

14. Fold top and bottom corners to midline. Glue flaps down.

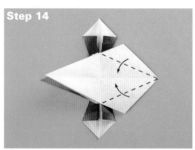

Step 15

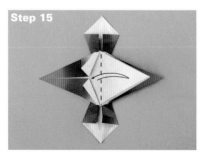

15. Fold and unfold.

Note: A craft stamen has been inserted down through the center of this posy.

BLOOMING STARFISH

NECESSARY ITEMS:

- Origami paper: 6", patterned
- Craft scissors

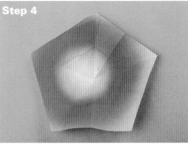

NECESSARY FOLDS:

1. Begin with pentagon base. Refer to Pentagon Base on page 26.

2. Make mountain and valley folds as indicated.

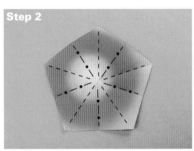

3. Fold tip to top edge. Unfold.

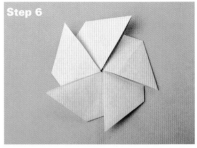

4. Open.

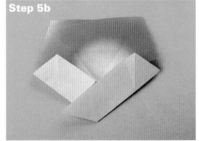

5. Fold bottom to center crease line. Make a mountain fold and bring it toward you as you fold the next side in.

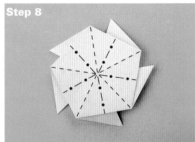

6. Repeat Step 5 on the next side. Continue until all five sides are folded.

7. When folding the last corner, lift the first flap and fold over the last, reversing the creases.

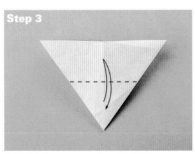

8. Turn model over. Make mountain and valley folds as indicated.

9. Bring tips of two petals together. Repeat for remaining sides to flatten.

100

BLOOMING STARFISH CONTINUED ▶

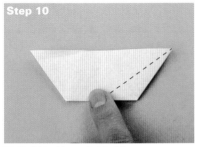

Step 10

10. Fold bottom-right side.

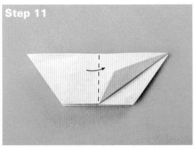

Step 11

11. Fold the tip of left layer over to right side.

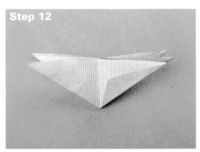

Step 12

12. Repeat Steps 10–11 for remaining layers.

Step 13

13. Fold center down to crease line, making a wide "V" shape crease. Repeat for remaining layers.

Step 14

14. Shape petals.

Step 15

15. Using craft scissors, diagonally cut off each petal tip.

Step 16

16. Completed Blooming Starfish.

Note: **Close-up of Blooming Starfish.**

CYCLAMEN FLOWERS

NECESSARY ITEMS:

- Origami papers: 6", solid for flower, 2", double-sided for calyx
- Acrylic paints: fuchsia (optional); yellow
- Floral spray paint: fuchsia (optional)
- Green floral tape
- Paintbrush
- Paper towel strip

NECESSARY FOLDS:

1. Begin with pentagon base. Refer to Pentagon Base on page 26.

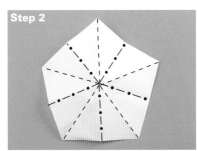

2. Fold as shown to flatten.

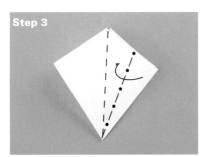

3. Fold right corner to vertical midline. Repeat for remaining layers.

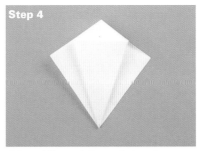

4. Insert finger into pocket and move pocket over to vertical midline. Repeat for remaining layers.

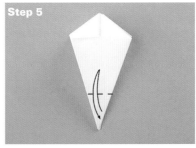

5. Fold and unfold as shown. Make certain to crease firmly.

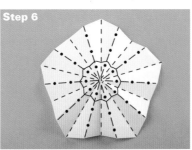

6. Open. With center facing up, fold each crease as shown to flatten.

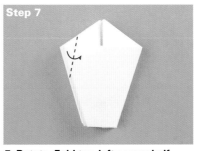

7. Rotate. Fold top-left corner half way to vertical midline.

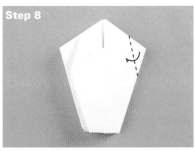

8. Fold top-right corner half way to vertical midline.

9. Repeat Steps 7–8 for remaining layers.

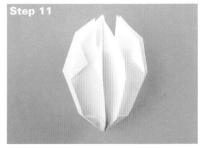

10. Fold bottom-left and bottom-right corners as indicated. Repeat for remaining layers.

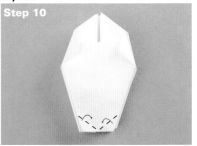

11. Open.

Note: For a fuchsia cyclamen flower as shown above, paint the flower base after Step 10, then spray-paint the flower after Step 11.

102

CYCLAMEN FLOWERS CONTINUED ▶

NECESSARY FOLDS FOR CALYX:

1. Begin with square pocket base. Refer to Square Pocket Base on page 22.

Step 2

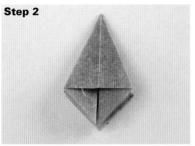

2. Fold left and right sides to vertical midline. Repeat for remaining layers.

3. Insert finger into pocket and move pocket to midline. Repeat for remaining layers.

Step 4

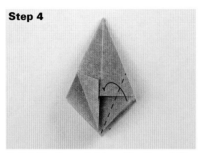

4. Fold bottom-right and bottom-left corner to vertical midline. Repeat for remaining layers.

Step 5

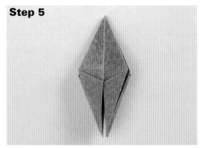

5. Completed calyx.

ASSEMBLING CYCLAMEN:

1. Apply glue onto one end of stem wire. Wrap small strip of paper towel around one end of stem wire.

2. Paint strip of paper yellow for stamen.

3. Wrap wire with floral tape.

Step 4

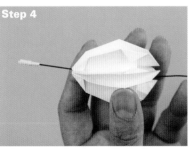

4. Insert nonstamen end of wire through flower.

Step 5

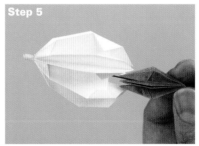

5. Insert calyx onto wire.

Step 6

6. Completed Cyclamen Flower.

CYCLAMEN BUD

NECESSARY ITEMS:

- Origami paper: 3", solid
- Glue stick
- Floral stem wire
- Floral paint spray: fuchsia (optional)
- Green floral tape

NECESSARY FOLDS:

1. Begin with the square pocket base. Refer to the Square Pocket Base on page 22.

Note: For a painted cyclamen bud as shown above, spray paint the bud after Step 4 below.

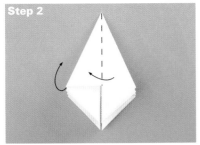

Step 2

2. Fold left and right sides to vertical midline. Insert finger into pocket and move pocket to midline.

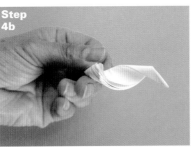

Step 3

3. Rotate. Move right side to left side. Move back-left side to right side.

Note: No slits should be showing.

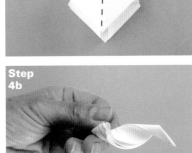

Step 4a

Step 4b

4. Fold in half vertically. Holding ends, twist.

5. Wrap wire with green floral tape.

6. Make Calyx. Refer to Calyx, Steps 1–4 on page 104.

7. Apply glue onto one end of stem wire.

8. Insert wire into bud. Twist bud around wire.

Step 9

9. Insert calyx into wire.

Step 10

10. Completed Cyclamen Bud.

105

PETUNIA KALEIDOSCOPE

NECESSARY ITEMS:

- Origami paper: 6", solid

NECESSARY FOLDS:

1. Begin with pentagon base. Refer to Pentagon Base on page 26.

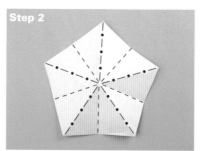

Step 2

2. Fold as indicated.

Step 3

3. Flatten.

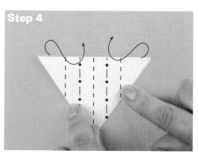

Step 4

4. Fold left and right sides to vertical midline. Unfold. Fold right side to left crease. Fold left side to right crease. Unfold.

Step 5

5. Insert finger into pocket.

Step 6a

Step 6b

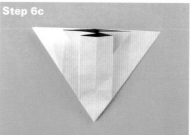

Step 6c

6. Push down, popping the tip up, making an inside reverse fold for both sides.

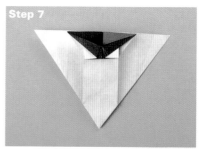

Step 7

7. Fold front flap down. Press open at edges. Repeat Steps 4–7 for remaining layers.

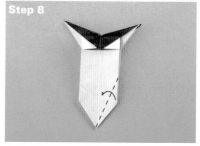

Step 8

8. Fold bottom-right corner to vertical midline. Repeat for remaining layers.

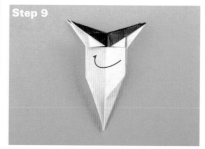

Step 9

9. Fold right side over left side. Repeat for remaining layers.

106

PETUNIA KALEIDOSCOPE CONTINUED ▶

12. Open flower.

13. Shape petals by pulling each petal downward.

14. Completed petunia.

Note: Craft stamens have been inserted down through the centers of these petunias.

MORNING GLORIES II

MORNING GLORIES II

NECESSARY ITEMS:

- Origami paper: 6", patterned
- Curling tool
- Stem wire with stamen

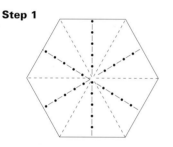

NECESSARY FOLDS:

Step 1

Step 4

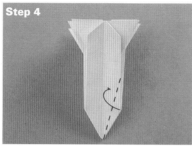

4. Fold bottom-right corner to vertical midline. Repeat for remaining layers.

Step 6

6. Insert craft stamen down through the center flower.

1. Begin with hexagon base. Refer to Hexagon Base on page 24.

2. Follow Petunia Kaleidoscope Steps 2–6 on pages 106–108. Repeat for all layers.

Step 5

5. Open flower by pulling petals downward. Using curling tool, curl petals.

Step 7

7. Completed Morning Glory II.

Note: If a curly stem is desired, make certain to use a craft stamen without wire. Curl bottom of stem around the shaft of a ballpoint pen.

Step 3

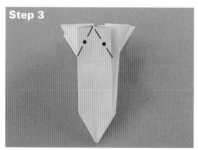

3. Fold right- and left-front flaps back as indicated. Repeat for remaining layers.

Note: Close-up of Morning Glories II.

NECESSARY ITEMS:

- Origami paper: 4" solid
- Fine-tipped black marker

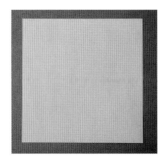

NECESSARY FOLDS:

1. Follow Petunia Kaleidoscope Steps 1–6 on page 106–108. Repeat for all layers.

Step 2

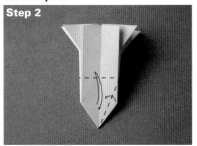

2. Fold in half and unfold to horizontal midline. Fold bottom-right side to vertical midline. Repeat for remaining layers.

Step 3

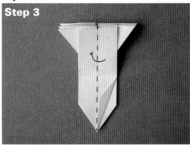

3. Fold right flap over to left. Repeat for remaining layer.

Step 4

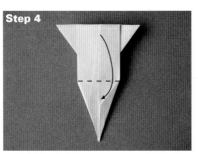

4. Fold front flap down.

Step 5

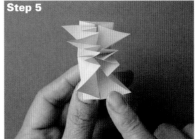

5. Pull both sides to open flower.

Step 6a

Step 6b

6. Make certain that each new petal starts on the top-right edge of previous petal.

Step 7

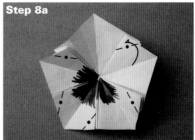

7. Using fine-tipped black marker, create center of pansy.

Step 8a

Step 8b

8. Make inside reverse fold at petal edges as indicated.

112

9. Open corner.

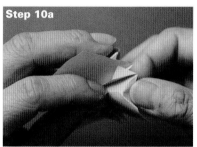

10. Fold back flap back. Make inner reverse fold at corners. Fold petals under.

11. Fold center flap forward. Repeat for each corner. Fold remaining flap forward, creating inside reverse fold.

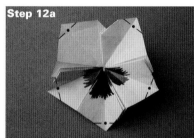

12. Fold each petal tip down as indicated.

13. Completed pansy.

Note: Close-up of Potted Pansies.

Note: These pansies have a craft stamen inserted down through the center instead of painting the centers.

ROSE BOUQUET

NECESSARY ITEMS:

- Origami paper: 4½", double-sided
- Glue stick

Note: **This project is very advanced. Practice with lightest weight origami paper that you can find before folding with the double-sided origami paper.**

NECESSARY FOLDS:

Note: **Origami paper with a different color on each side was used to better illustrate the folds. However, the usage of double-sided paper of the same color is recommended.**

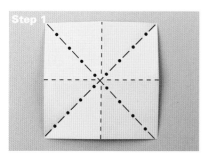

1. **Fold in half. Unfold. Rotate. Fold in half again. Unfold. Turn model over. Fold and unfold in half diagonally in both directions.**

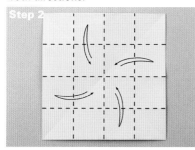

2. **Fold bottom to horizontal midline. Unfold. Rotate. Repeat for all sides.**

Note: **This will create a total of 16 squares.**

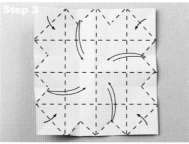

3. **Fold bottom to top crease line. Fold bottom-left and bottom-right corners to next immediate crease line. Unfold. Rotate and repeat for all sides. Fold all corners to first immediate fold. Do not unfold. Turn model over.**

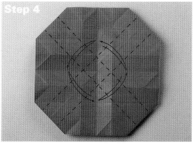

4. **Fold bottom-left side to top crease line of opposite side. Unfold. Rotate. Repeat on remaining smaller sides.**

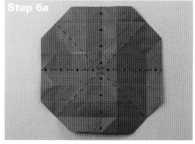

5. **Fold bottom side to next immediate top crease line. Unfold. Rotate. Repeat on all remaining larger sides.**

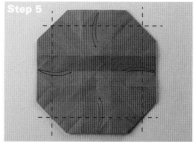

6. **Turn model over. Fold as shown to flatten. Fold left side forward as shown, making certain top corner resembles an outside reverse fold. Collapse into triangle pocket base.**

115

ROSE BOUQUET CONTINUED ▶

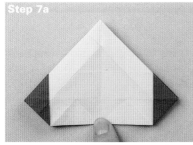

Step 7a

Step 9

9. Gently push down tip into square shape. Flatten. Turn model over.

Step 13

13. Move triangle to left. Repeat on remaining sides.

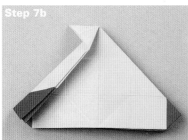

Step 7b

7. Fold top-right side back as shown. Fold top-left side forward as shown, making certain top corner resembles an outside reverse fold.

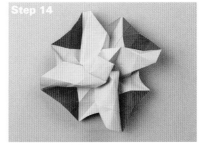

Step 10

10. Fold as shown.

Step 14

14. Turn model over.

Step 8a

Step 11

11. Open and fold as indicated, creasing up two creases.

Step 15

15. Fold down as shown.

Step 8b

8. Gently open, keeping reverse fold together.

Step 12

12. Bring bottom-right corner to fold crease.

117

16. Pull to left and tuck in.

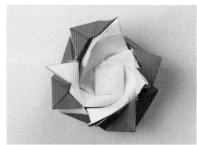

Note: Bottom view of the rose.

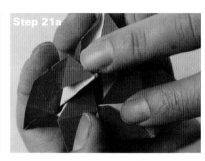

Step 21a

17. Fold as shown.

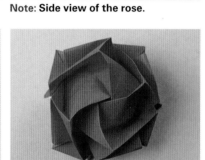

Note: Side view of the rose.

21. Tuck in the last tip.

18. Fold up as shown.

Note: Top view of the rose.

22. Turn model over. Shape and curl petals.

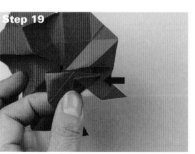

19. Fold bottom-right corner up and back. Repeat on remaining sides.

Note: Glue can be used to secure.

Step 20

20. Fold tips into center.

Step 23

23. Completed rose.

Note: These roses were folded slightly different from the Rose Bouquet on pages 115–118. Once the basic folds for a certain flower are learned, use your imagination and make it your own.

SUNSHINE LILIES

NECESSARY ITEMS:

- Origami paper: 6", patterned
- Curling tool
- Marking pen, round tip: brown
- Glue stick

NECESSARY FOLDS:

1. Begin with a square pocket base . Refer to Square Pocket Base on page 22.

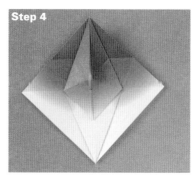

4. Crease along dashed lines. Unfold. Push left and right sides of resulting triangle to center of model and press to flatten.

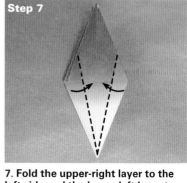

7. Fold the upper-right layer to the left side and the lower-left layer to the right side.

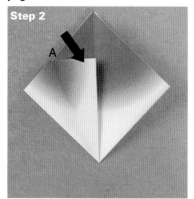

2. With opening at the top of the model, fold left-upper corner to vertical midline. Unfold.

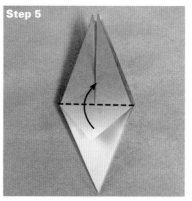

5. Turn model over and repeat Steps 2–4 for each side corner.

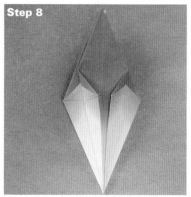

8. Fold lower-left and right sides to vertical midline.

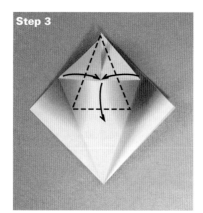

3. Insert finger into pocket and move pocket to center. Press to flatten.

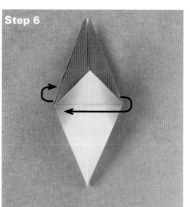

6. Fold bottom flap up. Repeat for each side.

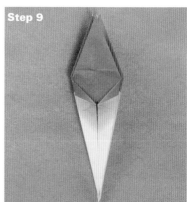

9. Turn model over and repeat for each side.

120

SUNSHINE LILIES CONTINUED ▶

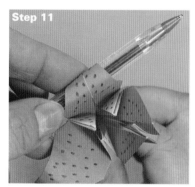

10. One at a time, pull each petal downward and dot over the surface, using marking pen.

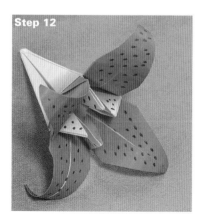

11. Open flower by pulling petals downward and curling them under, using the shaft of a ballpoint pen.

12. Completed lily.

Note: A silk flower pistil and stamen has been inserted down through the center of the lily.

Note: The above flowers are lilies with six petals developed by Soonboke Smith.

ABOUT THE AUTHOR

Soonboke Smith was born in Taejon, Korea; one of four children in her family. She grew up watching her mother work with pieces of old fabric—cutting them, folding them, and hand-stitching them together again, transforming them into new finely crafted garments. This time with her mother would later spark Soonboke's interest in Korean Jong ie Jup Gi, or paper folding.

In 1992, Soonboke moved to the United States. She is currently living in Roy, Utah. She has a 12-year-old daughter, Samantha, who is turning out to be quite an origami artist herself. They are proud of their Korean culture and the heritage they share.

Soonboke is an origami instructor at Michael's Crafts store in Riverdale, Utah. During the summer, she teaches an origami day camp for children at the Eccles Community Art Center in Ogden, Utah. She has also worked as a Korean Language teacher and as a substitute teacher at her daughter's elementary school. The children love it when she uses origami as part of her lesson plan.

Some of Soonboke's hobbies include drawing, singing, and working out. She finds that these activities, like origami, all help her to relax. Origami has allowed her to expand her creativity and has taught her patience.

DEDICATION

This book is dedicated to my mother whose constant love, support, and prayers sustain me in all that I do and all that I am. . . now and forever. I love you.

To my dear friend, Anthony Rojas, this book is also dedicated to you. Thank-you for your never-ending support and friendship through this wonderful endeavor and each and every day of my life.

Thank-you to all the people, who took the time to read and purchase my book. You are supporting me in making my dream come true. I hope that I have helped you to discover the creative artist within yourself.

SPECIAL THANKS

To Cindy, thank-you for giving me the good news about authoring a second book with Chapelle, Ltd. It is great working with you. To Jo, thank-you for allowing us the usage of live plants when creating the floral arrangements. It made my work look more beautiful and like a true work of art. To Martin Lovato, the showroom design manager at Jimmy's Floral, thank-you for the use of your creative artist talents. To Ryne, Justin, and Suzy, thank-you for all of your hardwork on the photography for this book. It was a pleasure working with each of you. To Kim, thank-you for all the work you did on this book and making my hands, look 20 years younger. To Desirée, thank-you for going the extra mile for me and for always being there when I needed you. You are awesome for making the time for me in your very busy schedule. To Karmen, thank-you for listening to any suggestions and ideas that I may have had.

To Kim Nam Joon and my Jeoung Up ward in Korea, thank-you for your help with the flowers featured in this book. This book would not have been possible without your helping hands. To Dr. Virginia Mol, thank-you for your continuous support and en-couragement on this book. You are a great doctor and dear friend.

A special thank-you to Nathiel-Rojas, who is like a son to me. Thank-you for sacrificing your room for me and my origami flowers and for not complaining when you would come over to visit. To my daughter, Samantha, thank-you for believing in me and supporting me with your constant prayers.

METRIC CONVERSION CHART

mm-millimetres   cm-centimetres
inches to millimetres and centimetres

inches	mm	cm	inches	cm	inches	cm
⅛	3	0.3	9	22.9	30	76.2
¼	6	0.6	10	25.4	31	78.7
⅜	10	1.0	11	27.9	32	81.3
½	13	1.3	12	30.5	33	83.8
⅝	16	1.6	13	33.0	34	86.4
¾	19	1.9	14	35.6	35	88.9
⅞	22	2.2	15	38.1	36	91.4
1	25	2.5	16	40.6	37	94.0
1¼	32	3.2	17	43.2	38	96.5
1½	38	3.8	18	45.7	39	99.1
1¾	44	4.4	19	48.3	40	101.6
2	51	5.1	20	50.8	41	104.1
2½	64	6.4	21	53.3	42	106.7
3	76	7.6	22	55.9	43	109.2
3½	89	8.9	23	58.4	44	111.8
4	102	10.2	24	61.0	45	114.3
4½	114	11.4	25	63.5	46	116.8
5	127	12.7	26	66.0	47	119.4
6	152	15.2	27	68.6	48	121.9
7	178	17.8	28	71.1	49	124.5
8	203	20.3	29	73.7	50	127.0

INDEX

Accordion Folds 19

Base Forms 20–29

Basic Folds 19

Basic folds, basic forms 14

Beautiful Blossoms 64–65

Blooming Flowers 58–123

Blooming Petals 30–57

Blooming Starfish 99–101

Charming Anemonies 66–67

Color Spots 69–71

Crazy Cosmos 42–44

Crease, or Fold & Unfold 15

Crease, precrease 14

Curling 14

Cut 15

Cute Clovers 56–57

Cutting Tools 12

Cyclamen Bud 105

Cyclamen Flowers 102–104

Decorative-edged Scissors 12

Delicate Bellflowers 77–79

Enchanting Posies 96–98

Elegant Irises 60–62

Fingers 13

Fixatives & Sealers 13

Flower Fireworks 53–55

Fold Behind & Mountain Fold 15

Fold in Front & Valley Fold 15

Fold Over & Fold Back, or Pleat Fold 16

Fold Over & Over 16

General Instructions 10–29

Giving Thanks 32–33

Glue 13

Hand-held Rotary Cutter 12

Hexagon Base 24

Ice Cream Base 20

Inflate 16

Insert or Pull Out 16

Inside Reverse Fold 17

Introduction 8

Key for Symbols 15–17

Long Triangle Base 28

Lovely Lilies 63

Making a Sharp Crease 18

Mat Base 21

Measuring & Shaping Tools 12

Measuring Sticks 13

Metric Conversion Chart 126

Morning Glories 82–84

Morning Glories II 109–110

INDEX CONTINUED ▶

Mountain Fold 14, 19

Necessary Items 10–13

Octagon Base 25

Orange Twinkles 93–95

Origami Papers 10–11

Outside Reverse Fold 17

Pentagon Base 26

Perfect Peonies 38–40

Periwinkle Adaptation 89

Periwinkle Patch 85–87

Petunia Kaleidoscope 106–108

Pinwheel Daisies 47–49

Place Finger Between Layers 17

Poppies Forever 34–35

Potted Pansies 111–113

Press or Push In 17

Pretty Petals 72–73

Previous Position 16

Purple Stars 36–37

Pushing Tools 13

Rose Bouquet 115–118

Rotary Trimmer 12

Rotate the Model 16

Scissors 12

Score, scoring 14

Scoring Blades & Bone Folders 13

Spring Tulips 74–76

Square Pocket Base 22

Star Flowers 45–46

Starburst Dahlias 90–92

Sunshine Lilies 120–122

Sweet Carnations 50–52

Terms to Know 14–15

Triangle Base 29

Triangle Pocket Base 23

Turn Model Over 15

Valley Fold 14, 19

Vivid Violets 80–81